the Money *Conversation*

Speak the Truth.

Set the Standard.

Get Paid Without Apology.

LINDA A. HUNT

Published by Six Scrolls, Monroe, Connecticut

www.sixscrolls.com

ISBN 978-0-9986492-1-4 (paperback)
ISBN 978-0-9986492-0-7 (eBook)
Library of Congress Control Number: 2026901358

To my inner circle—

You held me through the hardest parts.

You watched me heal.

*And you celebrated me before
the pages were finished.*

*This book isn't just a milestone;
it's a mirror of what your love made possible.*

Contents

Directory of Scripts

Chapter 1: Pricing as Power

Chapter 2: Raise Your Prices Without Asking Permission

Chapter 8: Off-Boarding is Leadership

Bonus Scripts for Sticky Situations

Acknowledgments

This book may have come through my hands alone, but it was never a solo effort.

To my inner circle: Thank you for holding me through the hard seasons, witnessing my healing, and celebrating me long before this was finished. You didn't just cheer me on, you reminded me who I was when I forgot.

To every client whose sticky moment gave this book its heartbeat: Thank you for showing me where clarity was needed, and for proving that boundaries can be both loving and firm.

And to the ones who challenged me to speak up— even when it felt risky—this book is what happened when I finally did.

The Money Conversation
Invocation

Before you begin, pause.

Breathe in through your nose.
Hold.
Breathe out through your mouth.
Again.
One more time.

You are not just about to read a book.
You are entering a sacred conversation.
One you've avoided, desired, resisted, and craved.
One that doesn't just change your bank account—
it changes your relationship to power.

This isn't about numbers.
It's about narratives.
The ones you inherited.

The ones you created.
And the one you're ready to rewrite.

Let this be your turning point.
Not with urgency.
But with truth.

You are safe to open.
You are ready to remember.
And you are worthy to receive.

Let the Money Conversation begin.

A Note on Language: What I Mean by "Field"

You'll see me use the word "field" throughout this book. When I say, "your field," I'm not talking about your career, your background, or your network.

I'm talking about the invisible energetic frequency you carry—the one that speaks before you say a word.

Your field is made up of:

- Your nervous system regulation,
- Your emotional patterns,
- Your thoughts and beliefs,
- Your lived experiences, and
- The Soul-coded truth beneath all of it.

Your field communicates how available you are to receive.

It tells the world what is *normal* for you—financially, relationally, energetically.

The Money Conversation isn't just about what you say. It's about what your field *permits*. This book teaches you how to calibrate your words *and* your energy, so you're no longer contradicting yourself in silence.

Start Here: Download Your Copy of *The Money Conversation Scriptbook*

Want every script from this book in one easy place? Scan the QR code to download your copy of *The Money Conversation Scriptbook*, your complete collection of every pricing and boundary script from the book.

When you sign up, you'll also receive "The SUM: Pricing, Profit & Power"—a no-fluff, practical newsletter delivered to your inbox once a month to help you speak the truth, set the standard, and get paid without apology.

Why Money Conversations Feel So Damn Hard—and How That Ends Here

f you've ever hesitated to send an invoice, felt your stomach tighten when a client pushed back on your price, or discounted your work just to avoid the discomfort, you're not broken. You're not alone. If your body contracts around money, there's a disconnect worth correcting.

And I'd be willing to bet you *are* undercharging.

It's not because you don't know your worth. It's because the line between you and your work has been blurred.

When your service is your presence, your voice, your heart, it's hard to name a number without feeling like you're pricing yourself.

I know that blur. I've lived it.

Pricing isn't about worth. It's about *value clarity*.

And no one ever taught you how to *name* it. Out loud. On purpose. Without flinching.

Most of us inherited invisible scripts like:

- Don't talk about money.
- Be grateful for the work.
- If you charge too much, you'll lose them.

And so we learned to shrink, soften, second-guess.

Somewhere along the way, we got it twisted. We confused discounting with generosity.

Avoidance with grace.

Politeness with professionalism.

> **But here's the truth: Avoiding money conversations is costing you—literally.**

Not just income.

But clarity. Boundaries. Self-trust.

This book is here to end that.

Confidence Isn't a Negotiation. It's a Frequency.
Most people think pricing is about negotiation—haggling until both sides "feel okay."

Let's cut that noise.

When you're clear on your value and grounded in your process, you don't negotiate—you calibrate.

You attract aligned clients who don't need convincing.

You communicate with clean, anchored clarity.

You hold your standards without apology.

I once had a client who prided herself on always negotiating—especially with service providers. The farther she was from the problem, the more liberty she felt to bargain. It made her feel smart. Strategic.

The only time she didn't "win"? When in negotiation with a landlord who calmy and confidently returned to his value, his process, again and again. No power struggle. No emotional hook. Just clarity. Just frequency.

That's the energy of pricing from power. It doesn't need to defend itself—it just holds.

The Right Words Change Everything

You don't need a script. You need a spine.

The right script doesn't replace your power—it returns you to it.

When your nervous system braces, your voice can wobble—not because you're weak, but because your body is preparing for war.

That's why structure matters.

> **A script isn't a crutch. It's a coded reminder of your leadership.**

It helps your body stay in the room until your power becomes second nature.

Inside this book you'll learn how to:

- Handle pricing objections without flinching.
- Set boundaries without guilt.
- Stand in the value of your work—without apology, over-explaining, or shrinking.

Because once your language matches your energy, everything clicks.

From Underselling to Unapologetic

I didn't plan to start a business.

I left the corporate world burned out, jumped without a net, and landed in entrepreneurship because I couldn't not help.

It started with a bookkeeping favor. But what I was actually doing was:

- Rebuilding operations.
- Redesigning systems for small businesses.
- Coaching pricing.

Holding entire backends together—quietly.

And I was charging by the hour—like a side hustle.

The faster I worked, the less I earned.

The more I mastered, the more invisible I became. Because I hadn't yet owned the transformation I delivered.

Because I didn't yet see myself as a strategist in what I delivered. I called it bookkeeping, but it was business recalibration.

That misrepresentation shaped everything.

Until one day a client's wife casually started running my schedule—because I hadn't.

Not because she was rude—but because I had set no boundary, no standard, no voice.

This wasn't her fault. It was mine.

She saw me as support staff, not a strategist, because that's how I was presenting myself.

Everything Changed When I Stopped Selling Time and Started Selling Truth

I stepped back.

Rebuilt my process.

Renamed the transformation I was delivering.

This time?

I stopped working to prove I was enough. I started offering what created results:

- Structure
- Strategy
- Outcomes

I stopped apologizing for my prices.

I didn't just charge more; I charged in alignment with what my work created.

It didn't feel natural at first.

Years of undercharging had trained my nervous system to flinch at being fully seen.

But every repetition, the truth held.

And when it did?

So did my clients.

I wasn't merely a provider.

I was the authority.

This Book Isn't About Selling, It's About Sovereignty.

This isn't about sales tricks or polished pitches.

It's about remembering who you are.

Owning what you bring.

And commanding a room—without raising your voice.

> **You're not here to chase clients.**

You're here to lead them.

Let's begin.

CHAPTER 1

Pricing as Power

remember this moment like a frequency shift. I was in a private session with two clients.

One of them had been quietly questioning her prices for months.

During a simple recalibration exercise, she made one adjustment.

Her shoulders dropped. She exhaled.

"Now I don't have to move out of the country when I retire," she said.

That moment didn't change her numbers, but changed her future.

Within months, she took a bold leap she'd resisted for years—she bought a business she never believed she could own.

> Pricing isn't arithmetic. It's energetic reckoning with how fully you're willing to be seen.

Energetic Block This Chapter Clears

The belief that talking about money is rude, shameful, or confrontational.

What You're Repatterning

You learned to people-please. You learned to downplay. You learned to equate avoiding the money conversation with being "gracious."

But grace without clarity isn't sovereignty.

This chapter breaks that loop.

Field Calibration Before You Begin

Pause.

Breathe.

Let your nervous system know that nothing about speaking your value is a threat.

This isn't confrontation. This is congruence.

You are about to learn how to communicate about money with sovereignty, warmth, and clean, energetic lines.

And once you do—you won't go back.

Because when pricing feels threatening to you, it's rarely about the number.

It's about how safe you feel being seen in your value.

What Not to Do

- *Don't wait until it's awkward.* If money hasn't been discussed, the problem isn't the client—it's your avoidance.
- *Don't assume clarity exists because you feel clear.* If it's not said out loud, it's not real.
- *Don't default to email when a conversation is required.* If the exchange involves energy, voice is required.

How to State Your Price With Confidence and Clarity

Pricing isn't the first thing you say. But when it's time to say it, your words matter. Clients don't just want a number. They want to feel what that number represents.

Here's the truth. People aren't buying your time—they're buying your *process*, your *perspective*, and your *pathway* to results. And the clearer you are about how you work, the easier it is for them to trust the investment.

Before you state the price, ground the conversation in *how* you work:

> "We use a structured process to [insert big-picture result] by focusing on [insert key approach or method]. That ensures you get consistent, high-level outcomes every time. Based on that, the investment is $X."

That simple bridge, from process to price, creates safety. It shows them:

- You're not guessing.
- You've done this before.
- There's a framework holding the work.

This isn't about reciting a robotic pitch. It's about showing your certainty. When your words carry clarity, your price lands clean.

Script Examples: "Here's How Our Process Works—and Your Investment"

Use these as a framework, not a formula. Adapt the words to fit your tone, work, and process. The goal is to communicate clarity and confidence.

Bookkeeper/Operations Consultant

"We follow a structured process to streamline your systems and deliver clean, timely financials every month. That includes weekly bill pay, bank reconciliations, and monthly reporting— all customized to your internal flow. Based on that, the monthly investment is $X."

Web Designer/Creative Service Provider

"I work in three phases: discovery, design, and delivery. We start with a deep dive into your brand and goals, then move into iterative design, and wrap with implementation and launch support. The investment for this full process is $X."

Coach/Strategist/Consultant

> "This isn't just about sessions—
> it's a full recalibration. We follow a three-part
> framework: clarify your vision, upgrade your
> systems, and embed new patterns through
> ongoing coaching. That structured process is
> what drives results; the investment is $X."

Why These Work

These scripts position your offer inside a clear, contained structure, which instantly signals professionalism, boundaries, and value. You're not just naming a price, you're showing what justifies it. This removes ambiguity, builds trust, and makes it easier for your clients to say yes—without needing to be "sold."

How to Handle "That's Too Expensive!" Without Shrinking

First, know this: "Too expensive" rarely means *too much money.*

It means not enough *clarity.*

When clients push back on price, they're usually not trying to devalue you. They're trying to reconcile your number with their nervous system. What they're asking is:

- "Can I trust this?"
- "Will this work for me?"
- "Am I the kind of person who invests at this level?"

Don't spiral. Don't defend. Don't discount.

> **Above all, don't decide what someone else can afford.**

That's your money story talking, not theirs.

Your job is to stay clean in the conversation.

To hold the value.

To give them clarity, not coddling.

Script Option 1: Budget Constraints

WHY THIS WORKS

It preserves your value and your boundaries, without making them wrong for where they are.

Script Option 2: For Trust Concerns

WHY THIS WORKS

It reframes expensive as smart discernment, and gives a safe path forward without you chasing.

Reframing: Price as an Investment, Not an Expense

Before you internalize a client's money story, check your own.

Too many service providers lower their prices not because the value isn't there, but because they've been conditioned to see pricing as confrontation, not calibration.

But price isn't the problem. Unspoken value is.

Let's reframe what you're offering—and why it's worth standing in.

Underlying Belief

If I set a boundary, I'll upset the client—or lose them.

New Perspective

Your pricing reflects the transformation your service delivers—not the hours you log.

Mindset Shift

My service creates outcomes. The investment reflects what that's worth—not just what it costs.

Affirmation

I stand in the value of my work. I communicate my pricing with clarity, calm, and conviction.

When your clients understand the *result*, they stop fixating on the *rate*. You're not asking them to spend money.

You're inviting them to step into a result.

KEY TAKEAWAYS

1. *Clarity builds confidence.* Custom quoting leads to confusion. Clear, repeatable pricing signals: "I know what this is worth." That certainty is contagious.

2. *Anchor pricing in process.* You're not selling hours—you're delivering outcomes. Ground your price in a defined framework that shows how you get results.

3. *Budget objections aren't always about money.* When someone says "too expensive," they may be expressing doubt, fear, or past experience that

eroded trust. Meet that energy with calm clarity, not collapse.

4. *Offer structure, not discounts.* Hold your price. If needed, shift the scope. Offering a scaled-down version preserves value—and integrity.

5. *Not everyone is your client—and that's a good thing.* When a prospect keeps negotiating, they're not respecting your boundaries. That's not a fit— it's a flag. Let it be a clean "no."

CHAPTER 2

Raise Your Prices Without Asking Permission

still remember staring at the number I'd written down.

It wasn't outrageous. It wasn't even bold.

But it was higher than I'd ever charged and it made my stomach flip.

Not because the math was wrong. But because the moment felt like a risk.

- What if they said no?
- What if I was being greedy?
- What if this tiny stretch cost me the client?

> That's the thing about raising your prices. It's rarely about the number.

It's about what the number seems to say about *you*—what others will think and/or do. Will they remain your client? Will they become a client? Will they push back? Reject your proposal?

You've hit that edge where the math doesn't work and the model doesn't hold. You're delivering more for less—and it's costing you.

But you hesitate.

That hesitation isn't logic. It's legacy—inherited stories about what you're allowed to ask for, who you're allowed to be, and what's too much.

This chapter isn't about inflation. It's about evolution.

You'll learn how to raise your pricing with clean language, steady energy, and grounded authority so your business can grow sustainably, and your leadership can hold.

That's what we're here to name.

Not just the numbers, but the narratives.

Because raising your prices isn't a math problem.

It's an energetic reclamation.

Let's recalibrate.

Energetic Block This Chapter Clears

Outsourcing your authority. Believing money dictates your choices, your capacity, or your value.

What You're Repatterning

You've been told money is the problem. That it's the reason you feel pressure, guilt, shame.

But money isn't the source. It's the speaker.

It amplifies what's already present—power or insecurity.

This chapter puts the pen back in your hand. You write the terms now.

Field Calibration Before You Begin

Pause.

Breathe.

Drop into your body.

Feel your pricing not as a number, but as a standard.

Is your pricing holding its shape like a clean boundary you can trust?

Or is it hedging like an apology wrapped in a number?

Because this isn't about changing a rate.

It's about changing what you believe that rate says about you.

When your pricing rises from truth, not fear, your field stays clean, your power stays intact, and the right clients don't disappear—they lean in.

The Right (and Wrong) Way to Raise Your Prices

Yes, we are talking about it—raising prices! One of the most common mistakes service providers make is waiting too long to increase their prices. Some never do, fearing they'll lose clients. On the other hand, raising prices too frequently can create instability. The key is to strike a balance—pricing should be reviewed periodically based on business growth, inflation, and market shifts. Raising your prices can feel nerve-racking, but it is a necessary step to ensure your business remains sustainable and profitable. The key is to approach it strategically, communicating the change with confidence and clarity.

A poorly communicated price increase can cause unnecessary friction. Instead of positioning it as a request, confidently present it as a business decision that supports quality service. If you approach it with hesitation, clients may feel they have room to negotiate or question whether the increase is justified.

The right way to raise prices is to position it as a natural evolution of your business, reinforcing the value you provide. Pricing adjustments should be framed around improvements to your services, increased expertise, or market shifts that make it necessary. Clients who value your work will understand when they see the benefits of continuing to work with you.

What Not to Do

- *Don't fill the silence with stories.* Silence doesn't mean "no." It often means pause, processing, or power recalibrating. Let it breathe.

- *Don't chase energy that's already withdrawing.* That's not service; it's self-abandonment in disguise.
- *Don't soften your power to be liked.* When you lower your frequency to make your pricing feel safer, you lower the integrity of your work.
- *Don't treat price changes like apologies.* Growth doesn't need justification. It needs a boundary around the value of the results you deliver.

If raising your prices still feels like something you'll get to eventually, this chapter is for you.

Not because you should charge more.

But because you deserve to be supported by the business you're building.

For Those Who Have Not Raised Their Rates Yet

If you've never raised your prices, let's pause here. You're not alone.

Most service providers delay the shift far longer than they should. Not because they don't *know* it's time, but because they're waiting to feel ready.

To feel confident. To feel justified.

But here's the truth: You're not just undercharging. You're under-resourcing the business owner you came here to be.

Not just financially, but energetically. You're pouring out more than you're being replenished.

That's not sustainable. That's slow self-abandonment disguised as being nice.

I learned this the hard way.

At the time, I was billing hourly—and the better I got, the *less* I made. I was so efficient, it started feeling like I was being punished for being good at my job. Padding the invoice felt gross. Discounting felt worse.

I knew I needed to switch to a retainer model—something structured, clean, and consistent.

I mapped it all out. Practiced what I'd say. Got clear.

And then? I froze.

I called one client, secretly hoping they wouldn't answer.

They didn't.

I left the longest, most wobbly voicemail of my life. I over-explained. I apologized. I gave my power away in real-time.

And then? Nothing. No reply. Just silence.

That silence taught me something loud: When you over-explain, you unconsciously invite doubt. When you apologize for evolving, you signal uncertainty.

> **Clarity is holding the standard**
> ***without* looking for approval.**

You're not asking for permission to charge more. You're choosing to build a business that supports you—energetically, financially, and sustainably.

Because if your business only works when you over-deliver and undercharge, it doesn't work.

Script: Here's How We Price Our Work (For New Clients)

"Can you walk me through your pricing?"

"Absolutely. I've built a pricing structure that reflects the depth of work, the strategic support, and the outcomes we deliver. Based on the scope we've discussed, your investment would be [price or range]. If you're ready, I can walk you through how it breaks down and what it includes."

Script: Here's What's Changing and Why (For Existing Clients)

"I noticed your pricing is going up. What's changing?"

"I value our work together, and as my business evolves, I periodically review my structure to make sure the quality of service remains high. Over time, I've refined how I deliver results, and this adjustment reflects that. I wanted to give you a heads-up ahead of time. The new pricing will take effect on [date], and I'm happy to answer any questions about what's shifting."

How to Give Existing Clients a Price Increase Notice

When it comes to long-standing clients, a pricing shift can feel more tender—especially if you've outgrown the rate they came in on. The relationship is there. The loyalty is real. Yet the numbers no longer work.

> This isn't about repaying loyalty with discounts. It's about honoring the relationship with clarity.

If you've refined your offers, deepened your expertise, or shifted your scope, your pricing should evolve to reflect that. The right clients will understand. And the ones who don't? That's information.

To create a clean transition:

- Give thirty to sixty days' notice before implementing the change.
- Reaffirm the value you've delivered and what's improving.
- Offer space for a conversation, but don't invite negotiation.
- Lead with clarity, not apology.

Handling Pushback With Grace

Not every client will welcome a price increase with open arms. That's okay. Growth reveals alignment. It shows you who's on board and who's not meant to continue. Your job isn't to convince, but to calibrate.

Clients may hesitate for all kinds of reasons:

- Their own money stories
- Budget constraints
- Past experiences that made them wary

But here's what matters: Their reaction doesn't define your value. Your response does.

This is the moment to hold your standard without getting defensive, apologetic, or over-explaining. And definitely without making assumptions about what someone can or can't afford based on your own money story.

Think about it like this. Restaurants don't apologize when egg prices rise. They don't write heartfelt essays on the menu or beg diners to understand. They adjust. With clarity. Because the cost of ingredients changed.

The same is true for your work.

As your internal costs rise—experience, skillset, energetic output—your pricing adjusts. Not because you're asking for permission, but because you're honoring the truth of your business.

Script: "I Completely Understand Your Concerns. Here's What's Changing and Why."

WHY THIS WORKS

- You lead with generosity and grounded clarity, not justification.
- You hold the standard without making the client wrong.
- You redirect the conversation toward solutions, not scarcity.

Some clients may stay. Others may go. That's not rejection—it's recalibration. Growth doesn't require everyone to come with you. It merely requires that you don't abandon yourself on the way.

Reframing: Price Increases as a Natural Business Evolution

Holding your prices isn't just about language. It's about the internal recalibration that allows your nervous system to stay regulated—even when someone pushes back.

Because if you don't shift the belief system underneath your business, you'll keep reverting to the pattern.

Over-explaining. Underselling. Shrinking to keep the peace.

So, let's name what's really driving the discomfort.

Underlying Belief:

"If I raise my prices, clients will leave."

New Perspective:

Raising prices is a standard part of running a successful business. As you grow, refine your expertise, and improve your service offerings, your pricing should reflect that increased value. While price increases may lead to some client turnover, this is a normal and healthy part of business growth.

Mindset Shift

The right clients recognize my expertise and results. A price increase ensures I can continue delivering exceptional service while attracting those clients who appreciate my work.

Affirmation

I trust that my pricing aligns with the value I provide, and I welcome clients who respect my expertise and commitment to quality.

When your pricing reflects your power—not your people-pleasing—everything stabilizes. You're no longer waiting for permission, you're leading from clarity.

KEY TAKEAWAYS

1. *Raising your prices isn't just about math—it's about clarity.* Price increases aren't emotional. They're a natural expression of clarity in your value, your evolutions, and your standards.
2. *Lead with clarity, not apology.* When you present pricing shifts as grounded business decisions, not emotional confessions, you anchor trust and authority.
3. *Handle pushback with grace, not guilt.* Stay rooted. Acknowledge concerns without absorbing them. Hold your value without over-explaining.
4. *You're not asking for permission.* Pricing from power isn't about who stays or who leaves. It's about leading from a clear sustainable container that holds the transformation—not just the transaction.

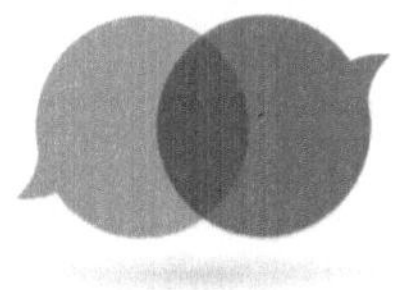

CHAPTER 3

How to Stop Scope Creep Without Losing the Client

When I first started my business, I had a law firm client I genuinely loved working with. We grew together. One of the partners, my financial contact, taught me a lot about how to serve well.

Nearly two years in, I was expanding my team—a huge milestone for my business. I sent out a thoughtful announcement letting clients know how we'd be structuring accounts moving forward.

The partner replied: "But you're still going to be doing all the work on our account, right?"

I responded with clarity: "I'll remain your financial contact, but the day-to-day work will now be handled by a team member I assign. I'll continue providing oversight, but we're operating with a team approach now."

He pushed back again, restating what he wanted.

I held the line—kindly and clearly. "Your account volume has grown. If you'd like me to personally handle all of it, your fee will increase by 50 percent. If we move forward with the team approach, your fee remains the same."

His reply? "Understood."

That moment taught me what so many service providers eventually learn the hard way: People will ask for what feels familiar. It's your job to hold what's sustainable.

> **You're not mean. You're leading.**

Boundaries in business are not rejection.

They're structure.

They're clarity.

They're not walls—they're agreements. Boundaries create mutual clarity so both parties know what's included, what's not, and how the work flows.

Confusing niceness with value only leads to resentment.

This chapter helps you spot the signs of *scope creep* early, name it clearly, and navigate it without guilt so you get paid fully, cleanly, and without apology.

Energetic Block This Chapter Clears

The unconscious belief that being liked is safer than being paid.

What You're Repatterning

This chapter expands your understanding of how often your people-pleasing tendencies masquerade as good service.

You're not only giving too much, you're relinquishing power.

We untangle the pattern of silence, self-sacrifice, and soft boundaries that quietly cost you more than any missed invoice ever could.

Field Calibration Before You Begin

Pause.

Take a deep breath.

Drop into your body.

Scan the last three client exchanges. Where did you collapse clarity to preserve comfort?

Where did you say *yes* when you meant, *that's extra*?

Where did you over-explain, delay, or undercharge to avoid discomfort?

This isn't about being harsh. It about being honest.

Boundaries aren't barricades. They're calibrated containers for your best work.

They don't push clients away. They bring the right ones closer, in a way that supports both you *and* them.

Once you see the pattern, you can name it.

And once it's named, it doesn't get to run the show anymore.

Spot It. Name It. Handle It.

Every service provider has been there. You start a project with clearly defined deliverables, and suddenly new requests start slipping in.

The client assumes it's included.

You know it's not.

This is scope creep. Left unchecked, it leads to unpaid work, strained boundaries, and quiet resentment.

Scope creep can show up in two ways:

1. Project-based, where extra requests keep stacking mid-project.
2. Ongoing/retainer-based, where the client's needs grow over time, but the scope and price never shift.

In both cases, the problem isn't always the ask.

It's the assumption.

Your job isn't to prevent clients from needing more. It's to name what's included and hold the line when it changes.

Clarity isn't confrontation. It's leadership. It's you taking the reins and steering the ship.

What Not to Do

- *Don't pretend you didn't notice.* Avoiding scope creep doesn't make it disappear, but rather delays the boundary breach.
- *Don't try to earn appreciation by absorbing extra work.* That's not generosity. That's martyrdom. It teaches clients that your time is elastic.
- *Don't retroactively defend your value.* If you didn't name the boundary upfront, you gave permission for it to blur. But you can still clean it up—without shame or story.

Spotting Scope Creep Before It Becomes a Problem

Scope creep almost never announces itself.

It tiptoes in.

An *urgent* tweak here.

A *quick favor* there.

A few extra deliverables that weren't in the contract—but felt too small to flag.

Until suddenly, your calendar is jam-packed without a moment to spare. And when you sit down to do your billing, you realize you're knee-deep in unpaid work.

That's how boundaries blur.

Not with one giant ask.

But with slow, steady erosion of clarity.

Scope creep often sounds like:

- Can you just . . . ?
- It'll only take a second.
- We assumed this was included.
- We didn't realize that was extra.

Or—if you work with a client on an ongoing basis— what used to take you four hours a week is now taking double that, quietly expanding without a single conversation.

If you're someone who cares deeply about doing good work, it's tempting to say yes.

But what starts as helpfulness quickly becomes an energetic leak—one that drains your time, your profit, and your trust in the client relationship.

Let's make this tangible.

Example: A Designer's Experience With Scope Drift Mid-Project

You're hired to design a logo and brand guidelines.

The contract clearly states: three initial logo concepts, two revision rounds, and a finalized color palette.

But then the emails start:

- "Can we get a version for Facebook banners?"
- "Would you mind mocking up a quick Instagram template?"

- "Could you do a draft of our email signature?"

At first, it feels easy enough to oblige.

But now you've doubled the project time—without doubling the pay.

Not because they were malicious. Because the boundary was never clearly re-stated when the scope shifted.

Script: Addressing Scope Creep Early (Without Tension)

> "I wanted to touch base about this request. Based on our initial agreement, this falls outside our original scope. I'd love to discuss how we can move forward with it as an additional service."

Alternative Script: Upleveling to a Larger Package

> "When we originally discussed your needs, these additional requests weren't part of the scope we outlined, which is why I initially recommended Package A. But based on where we're headed, Package B is a better fit. There will be an additional cost of $X. Let me know how you'd like to proceed."

WHY THIS WORKS

These kinds of conversations don't push clients away. They anchor trust, because they show you're more than a doer.

> You're a business owner with a process.

Example: A Bookkeeper's Experience With Scope Creep in Recurring Work

You're a bookkeeper hired to reconcile and deliver clean monthly financials.

But somewhere along the way, you started:

- Managing vendor payments
- Tracking accounts receivable
- Analyzing variances

You know the scope has grown. You *know* the rate no longer makes sense. But instead of saying something, you freeze.

Not because the work is small.

But because the story in your head is louder than the truth in your business.

"They'll think I'm greedy."
"They'll be annoyed if I bring it up."
"It's not that much more. I can manage."

This isn't just about extra tasks, it's about whether the energetic agreement between you and your clients still reflects the reality of the work.

Here's the script you can use to name that scope shift clearly—without guilt, wobble, or over-explaining.

Script: Naming the Pattern and Proposing a Shift

> "As your business has grown, so have your bookkeeping needs. When we started, the focus was reconciliations and monthly reporting. Over time, we began handling accounts receivable, vendor payments, and financial analysis—all of which go beyond our original agreement. I want to make sure you're fully supported so I'm recommending we shift to Package [insert name]. We'll begin billing at the new rate starting next month."

WHY THIS WORKS

By addressing the expanded scope directly and professionally, you reinforce the value of your services while ensuring fair compensation.

These scripts keep the conversation neutral, solution-focused, and rooted in good business practices. Most clients aren't trying to get something for free, they're simply asking. As business owners, it is our job to hold up the line. In my experience, every time I've named scope creep clearly, clients had no hesitation in paying more for what they were asking for.

Handling Additional Work Without Undervaluing Yourself

A client's growing needs are often your next growth opportunity—if you're willing to name it.

You don't have to wait for them to ask.

You can lead.

Spot the gap. Offer the upgrade. Anchor the value.

This isn't about pitching.

Stay one step ahead of their needs and show them you've already thought about what comes next.

Here's how that might look. You've been creating content for a client's social media. Their audience is growing. So is the volume of comments, direct messages, and requests.

Instead of waiting until they're overwhelmed, you offer a clean solution—exactly what they didn't know they were looking for.

Script: Proactively Offering a Solution

"I've noticed that managing responses and engagement on your posts has become more time-consuming as your audience grows. I'd love to offer a solution that supports consistency and momentum. I can take on engagement management as part of an upgraded package for an additional $X per month. Here's what that includes [brief description]. Let me know if that would be helpful, and we can update your service plan and set a start date."

WHY THIS WORKS

When you lead with clarity and care, you do more than protect your time—you elevate the relationship.

You position yourself not just as a provider, but as a strategic partner.

Saying No Without Feeling Guilty

Not every request deserves a yes.

Some things stretch your capacity.

Some things aren't in your zone of genius.

Some things simply don't align with the business you're building.

You're allowed to say no—without over-explaining, over-apologizing, or making yourself wrong for it.

Clear boundaries don't create conflict.

They prevent it.

> A professional "no" doesn't close doors, it builds respect.

Script: Saying No Professionally

> "That's not something I can accommodate within our current agreement [or something I don't offer]. If you'd like, I can refer you to someone I trust who may be able to help."

WHY THIS WORKS

This response is clean. Direct. Generous without self-sacrifice.

It doesn't leave space for negotiation. And that's the point.

Every no to what's misaligned is a yes to what sustains you.

You create space for what is.

Reframing: Boundaries Build Trust

If you've ever absorbed extra work instead of naming it, if you've ever delayed a hard conversation to keep things easy, or iff you've quietly over-delivered to avoid rocking the boat, you're not alone.

This isn't a failure in strategy.

It's a moment to realign your standards.

Boundaries aren't walls. They're good business and one way you demonstrate leadership.

They create the structure where clarity, respect, and trust can grow.

When your clients trust your clarity, they trust your work more too.

Let's shift the internal story so you stop associating boundaries with discomfort—and start seeing them as a core part of your value.

Underlying Belief

If I set a boundary, I'll upset the client—or lose them.

New Perspective

Clear boundaries don't break relationships. They strengthen them. When you name what's included (and what's not), you create mutual respect. Boundaries don't repel the right clients—they give them something to trust.

Mindset Shift

Boundaries aren't barriers. They're business clarity. When you stop seeing boundaries as conflict and start treating them as containers for your best work, everything changes.

Affirmation

I honor my time, energy, and expertise by naming what I'm available for and letting that clarity create deeper trust and alignment.

KEY TAKEAWAYS

1. *Scope creep is a clarity problem, not a client problem.* It's not that clients are taking advantage—it's that you haven't clearly defined the container. Boundaries are your responsibility.

2. *Set the standard early—and revisit it often.* Your services evolve. Your clients evolve. Make sure your scope and pricing evolve too. That's not confrontation, that's you strategizing and leading your business.

3. *When you address scope creep, you reinforce your value.* Naming what's extra doesn't make you difficult, it makes you trustworthy. Clarity shows you take both your work and your client's results seriously.

4. *Saying no is not a rejection, it's redirection.* You're not turning them away—you're turning them toward the right level of service. You are

honoring the level of support you deliver and its value.

5. *Boundaries don't push people away, they bring the right people closer.* Clients who value clarity are the ones who stay, grow, and refer. Boundaries don't diminish relationships. They solidify them.

CHAPTER 4

Your Price is Your Power

Money conversations used to make me squirm.

I loved talking about the work—what I saw, how I could help, what we could build together. But the moment pricing came up, I froze.

When I first started out, I charged by the hour. I'd walk a client through their entire scope of needs, then wait. Silent. Dreading the inevitable: "So, how much?"

Every invoice felt like a gamble.

- "Why did it take this long?"
- "Could this have been quicker?"
- "Can we review the hours?"

It was a disempowered pattern—unsustainable and exhausting.

That started to shift when I created a clear process for every initial conversation. I told myself it was for clarity. Truthfully? It was to ease *my* discomfort around money.

I began offering a paid evaluation. That one move changed everything.

It gave me space to lead the conversation instead of hiding in it. I was able to demonstrate my expertise while assessing a client's books, systems, and blind spots. In every evaluation, I covered:

- What needed immediate attention
- What would resolve the core issue
- What would elevate their financial clarity long term

From there, I quoted the fee—clean, clear, and unapologetic.

This wasn't pitch and pray. It was a solid business practice that enabled me to confidently lead the client.

No convincing. No bargaining. Just clarity.

Energetic Block This Chapter Clears

- Defaulting to defense, avoidance, or apology in money conversations.
- Relinquishing or diminishing your power because you're afraid to be too much or not enough.

What You're Repatterning

You're no longer waiting for permission to talk about money clearly, cleanly, and confidently.

This chapter calibrates you into a leadership posture—not by domination or force, but through self-trust and sacred clarity.

> **Money doesn't control the conversation. *You do.***

Not with manipulation.

But with coherence.

Field Calibration Before You Begin

Pause.

Breathe.

Close your eyes.

Call up a moment when someone challenged your pricing, delayed payment, or made a money comment that landed like a gut punch.

Notice how you responded.

Now notice what your body *wanted* to say.

This chapter gives that truth a voice.

Your Pricing Is a Boundary, Not a Bargaining Chip

Pricing your services confidently is one of the most important aspects of running a sustainable business. However, many service providers struggle when clients ask for discounts or push back on pricing. If you do not have a strategy for handling these conversations, you may find yourself undervaluing your work or making compromises that don't serve your business.

Here is the reality: You can navigate discount requests and negotiations with confidence while maintaining your value. These conversations are about much more than price—they are about positioning, perception, and setting clear expectations. When you handle them strategically, you reinforce your authority while ensuring your business remains profitable.

This chapter will guide you through setting firm pricing boundaries, responding to discounts professionally, and negotiating in a way that ensures fairness for both you and your clients.

Let me show you what that looks like in real life.

I anchored a new number that reflected the field I hold. When a new client approached me—someone who wanted to work directly with me, not my team—I saw the moment. I tripled my rate.

It felt audacious. My voice cracked when I named the number.

But I knew this project would demand more of my time and require an additional team member to supervise the work I'd usually oversee myself. It was a legitimate ask.

The client said yes without blinking.

And that relationship? It became one of the best I've ever had. I felt seen, valued, trusted. I contributed deeply to their company and was paid accordingly.

That taught me this: The right clients don't need convincing. They need clarity.

What Not to Do

- *Don't tiptoe.* If you're already dreading the money conversation, your field is wobbling and leaking power.
- *Don't explain your pricing like you're seeking permission.* You're not.
- *Don't lower your rate to avoid discomfort.* Discomfort is where your next level lives.

Holding your price is an energetic anchor, not a mere business decision. When you hold it with clarity, you collapse the space for negotiation, doubt, and scope creep.

Why Discounting Devalues Your Work

I still remember the first time a client asked for a discount because business was slow. As their accountant, I had full visibility into their numbers and knew the real story.

It put me in an awkward position.

I wanted to be empathetic.

But I also knew that discounting my rate would send the wrong signal.

> **Over time I learned this: Holding your rate is an act of self-respect.**

The clients who greatly value your work will rise to meet it.

Offering discounts might feel like the path of least resistance, but it's rarely a clean move. It teaches your clients that your prices are flexible, your boundaries negotiable, and your expertise up for debate.

As a service provider, you're selling your time—even if it's packaged. And time is a non-renewable resource.

Discounting can:

- Undermine the value of your work.
- Train clients to expect concessions.
- Make it harder to raise your rates in the future.
- Reduce profitability and increase resentment.

Instead of lowering your prices, explore how to adjust scope or add value in a way that protects your time and energy. For example:

- Offer a condensed version of the service focused on key deliverables.
- Add a resource or bonus that doesn't cost you extra time.
- Provide a payment plan that supports both parties.

Remember: If a client is already showing signs of being high maintenance, discounting won't change that dynamic. It'll only anchor you deeper into a relationship that asks more than it gives.

Now that we have explored the impact of discounting and client expectations, let's dive into how to respond professionally when a discount request comes up.

Script: Responding to a Discount Request

Here's the moment where many service providers default to justification, apology, or quick concessions. A confident response doesn't require defending your value—it requires holding your boundary.

You can say:

> "I don't offer discounts, but here's what I can do instead. We can explore a modified version of the service that fits your budget, or I can offer a flexible payment plan."

Why This Works

This response is clean. Clear. Professional.

It honors your pricing while offering the client an empowered next step.

I once had a client who asked for a discount because their "friend" charged less. I thanked them for the comparison and stood by my rate.

Instead of dropping the price, I offered a smaller scope.

They declined the smaller scope and accepted the original offer without edits, complaints, or hesitation. They could have gone with their friend. They didn't.

That moment confirmed that people respect clear pricing when it's delivered without apology.

And while you don't need to defend your pricing, you *can* negotiate—when it's done cleanly, consciously, and without compromise.

When (and How) to Negotiate While Maintaining Your Value

Negotiation isn't about lowering your standards, it's about finding alignment.

When done cleanly, it becomes a way to co-create solutions that honor the client's budget without compromising your boundaries.

The mistake most service providers make is assuming negotiation means *lowering the price*. It doesn't.

It means exploring options that maintain integrity on both sides.

Here are clean, empowered ways to negotiate:

- Adjust the scope to align with the client's budget.
- Offer a payment plan that maintains your rate.
- Add a non-time-intensive bonus that increases perceived value.

Notice what's not on the list: cutting your rate to close the sale.

If you want to meet a client where they are financially, do it without shrinking the value of what you provide.

Script: Uncovering the Client's True Concern
Sometimes price isn't the real objection—it's fear.

It's uncertainty.

It's a need for reassurance.

You can say:

> "I want to make sure this is the right fit for you. Are you concerned about the price itself, or is it more about making sure you get the level of support you need? Let's explore how we can structure this, so it aligns with both."

WHY THIS WORKS
This question brings the real issue into the open—without defensiveness or pressure. It repositions you as a collaborator, not a concession-maker.

And if that question uncovers a genuine budget constraint, you can still lead the conversation, without defaulting to discounts.

Script: Navigating a Budget Concern
When a client expresses a financial constraint, your job isn't to fix it, it's to lead them through it.

You can say:

> "I understand your budget constraints. Let's look at what we can adjust in the current package to keep the focus on what will deliver the strongest results."

WHY THIS WORKS

This keeps the conversation focused on outcomes—not cost. It reinforces your authority, protects your rate, and opens the door to aligned scope adjustments *without diluting your value.*

Setting Clear Payment Expectations

You now have structure.

Instead of reacting in the moment, you can default to clean, practiced language that holds your boundary and honors your client.

These scripts aren't just for sticky conversations, they're for calibration. Practice them—out loud, in front of a mirror, with a trusted peer—until they feel like muscle memory.

That's how you build confidence in money conversations.

Not by waiting for the discomfort to go away, but by preparing for it like the professional you are.

Now let's talk about what happens after the yes, because pricing is only part of the boundary.

Payment structure matters just as much.

One of the simplest ways to avoid pricing disputes is to set clear payment expectations before any work begins. Deposits. Due dates. Late payment policies.

These aren't terms—they're the energetic agreements that frame your field.

And when you state them clearly, without apology, you create trust from the start.

Clients don't want guesswork. They want to know what to expect. When payment terms are structured and upfront, you remove space for confusion, frustration, or drawn-out back-and-forth.

Many service providers hesitate to require deposits. But think about it: Hotels do. Event planners do. Lawyers do.

Why would your services be any different?

> **A deposit signals mutual commitment.**

It protects your time, reserves space in your calendar and energetically grounds the relationship before it begins.

Here's how I handle it:

> "I require a 50 percent deposit before starting any project. The remaining balance is due upon completion. For ongoing services, invoices are due within seven days of receipt."

It's simple. Clear. And nonnegotiable.

This keeps everything running smoothly and ensures both parties are equally invested from the start.

Script: Requiring a Deposit

> "I require a deposit before beginning work. This ensures that both of us are committed to the project and allows me to reserve time in my schedule. Here's how it works . . . "

WHY THIS WORKS

When you state this confidently, you're not being rigid, but professional. You're protecting your time, your energy, and the integrity of the work.

We'll go deeper into payment structure and how to hold the dynamic of a client relationship in the next chapter. For now, remember this: Clear terms create clean energy.

Reframing: Shifting Your Perspective on Discounts and Negotiations

Money conversations reveal what you believe about your work, your value, and your sovereignty—not just pricing.

If you've struggled to hold firm in these conversations, it's not because you're unprofessional or underprepared. It's because you were never taught that clarity is *enough*.

Let's rewire that now.

Underlying Belief

If I do not offer a discount, the client will go elsewhere.

New Perspective

Clients who truly value my work will respect my pricing. Discounting doesn't attract the right clients, it attracts those who prioritize cost over quality.

Mindset Shift

Standing firm in my pricing helps me build a business that's sustainable, profitable, and built on mutual respect.

Affirmation

I confidently charge what my work is worth, knowing my expertise delivers real value.

KEY TAKEAWAYS

1. *Discounting devalues your work.* It teaches clients to expect lower rates and undermines the value of your expertise.
2. *Negotiation doesn't mean lowering your price.* You can adjust scope, structure, or support without compromising your boundaries.
3. *Clarifying questions build trust and reveal the truth.* Often, clients need reassurance—not a discount. Ask before you assume.
4. *High-maintenance energy won't shift after the sale.* If a client is already pushing boundaries, a discount won't fix that dynamic.

5. *Clear payment expectations create clean relation-ships.* Deposits, due dates, and policies protect your time and build trust from day one.

56

CHAPTER 5

Getting Paid is a System, Not a Suggestion

For my first year in business, I didn't have a system for getting paid. I sent invoices, but I didn't have terms, timelines, or clear expectations.

Sometimes I'd start work with a deposit. Sometimes I'd let invoices sit for weeks before following up—telling myself I didn't want to seem pushy or money-obsessed.

And every time I did that, I paid the price:

- Unpaid invoices
- Discomfort I couldn't voice
- Not to mention a cashflow crunch

Getting paid isn't something you hope for. It's something you structure.

Handling pricing conversations is just one piece of the puzzle. The next challenge many service providers face is ensuring they get paid on time without uncomfortable follow-ups. In this chapter, we'll walk through how to set clear payment expectations, follow up on unpaid invoices professionally, and handle clients who delay—or refuse—to pay.

You're not alone if you've ever felt awkward about asking for payment.

Even seasoned professionals can find themselves tiptoeing, over-explaining, or delaying the follow-up— telling themselves they're being nice when what's happening is energetic leakage.

Before we restructure the system, let's name the field this chapter clears.

Energetic Block This Chapter Clears
- I don't want to be pushy about money.
- I hate following up on invoices.
- If I enforce my payment policy, I'll lose the client.

This chapter clears the fear of being too much or too rigid when it comes to receiving money. It interrupts the frequency of weak and blurry boundaries and money avoidance and restores your energetic authority around payment.

What You're Repatterning
This chapter invites you to shift from *hoping* you'll be paid on time to *ensuring* it. Your payment terms

are a boundary, a reflection of how much you honor your work, energy, and worth.

This is not just about invoicing—it's about coding your field with trust, clarity, and consistency.

Say what you do. Do what you say. No flinching. No fluff.

You're not just asking for money. You're leading the relationship.

Anchor the energy before a single dollar is exchanged.

Field Calibration Before You Begin

Pause.

Breathe.

Exhale.

Let your body land in the knowing that you are safe to speak about money—clearly, directly, unapologetically.

This isn't about confrontation. It's coherence.

You are the anchor for how money moves in your business.

You are not chasing payment—you are creating an energetic agreement rooted in clarity and mutual respect.

This chapter calibrates your nervous system to receive payment as the natural extension of your presence and your power.

Getting Paid Is a System, Not a Fluke

How you get paid isn't just an operational detail—it's your energetic infrastructure.

One of the fastest ways to drain your field is to get murky or passive around money. And for many service providers, this is exactly where they self-sabotage:

- Inconsistent payment terms
- Awkward follow-ups
- Loose expectations
- Policies that shift depending on the client.

It erodes authority. It invites boundary breaches. It signals energetic instability.

This chapter isn't just about collecting money.

It's about designing and upholding a simple, powerful payment system that protects your time, honors your value, and supports your business—energetically and financially.

Here's the truth: When payment expectations are clearly set and consistently enforced, they rarely get tested.

It's the energetic wobble—the passive-aggressive language, the delayed follow-ups, the "I'll just waive it this time"—that invites resistance.

Let's clean that up.

What Not to Do

- *Don't wait until the invoice is overdue before mentioning payment terms.*
- *Don't apologize for needing to follow up.*
- *Don't assume the client knows your process without having explicitly stated it.*
- *Don't bend your policy "just this once." That once teaches your clients how to treat you.*

Set the Frequency First

Your payment process isn't just admin—it's your energetic alignment in action.

Clients can feel when your boundaries are clear—and when they're porous. If you feel awkward about getting paid, that static will show up in the relationship.

When you're solid? They trust you more.

Start by locking in your structure with these tips:

- *Your payment terms are not fine print.* They're part of your energetic contract. State them confidently, in writing, and in every client interaction.
- *Decide when payment is due.* Is it 100 percent upfront? Fifty-fifty? Net fifteen? Whatever you choose, it must be *consistent*. The more you fluctuate, the more unstable your field becomes.
- *Include your terms everywhere.* Your client agreement. Your onboarding emails. The terms section of your invoice template. Repetition = regulation.

- *Choose your payment methods intention-ally.* ACH, card, invoicing software, payment plans—whatever keeps things clean and fric-tionless.
- *Set a sacred appointment with your money.* If you manage your own books, calendar weekly or monthly time to prepare, review, and follow up on billing. No skipping. No catching up later. If you wouldn't ghost a client, don't ghost your money.

This is about consistency, not control. When your structure is set, your frequency sharpens.

That's when getting paid becomes the natural con-clusion of your presence—not a separate hustle.

Now that your system is structured, let's ground it in language.

This isn't just about *what* you say—it's about *how* you hold it.

What does that mean? It's how you put the bound-aries and process you created into action. If you believe it, hold it—they will too.

Script: How My Payment Terms Work

"Here's how my payment terms work: I collect a 50 percent deposit to secure your start date, with the remaining balance due within five business days of completion. I send all invoices via [tool], and payments can be made via ACH or credit card. Let me know if you need help setting that up."

This is more than a logistics script, it's an energetic boundary.

You're not just informing the client—you're setting the tone for how your value will be received and respected from the beginning.

Do not begin work without the deposit in hand.

Not "promised." Not "processing." Paid. And landed.

I've made the mistake of starting work with only a signed agreement. Every time, I ended up in a costly leak of time and energy. Those were the clients who delayed payments, pushed boundaries, and drained my time. Why?

Because I bypassed my own structure.

I let the relationship open without an agreed-upon exchange, mutual respect.

That pattern repeated until I chose to interrupt it.

> **Lesson: When you wobble, your client mirrors the wobble.**

When you stand firm, they rise to meet you.

Let's move on to the next structure to put into place.

Follow Up Without Hesitation or Apology

If a payment is late, follow up immediately—and without drama. Neutrality is your power. Clarity is your leadership.

Most people avoid follow up because they don't want to seem needy or money-obsessed. This is about honoring the energetic agreement you already established, not needing money.

You provided a service. The client agreed to pay for it. Now you're simply anchoring the integrity of the exchange.

Automated reminders in your invoicing system can help, but don't default to canned language. Your message doesn't need to be cold, but it must be clear. Update the reminder text to reflect your tone and professionalism.

If the payment isn't received after that, don't send another email. Pick up the phone. Not a text. Not a nudge. A real conversation.

Script: Checking in on Payment

"Hey [Client Name], just following up on the outstanding invoice. I wanted to check in directly to make sure everything's clear on your end. Is there anything you need from me to move this forward?"

WHY IT WORKS

It holds mutual respect, opens space for a response, and gently reinforces expectation without pressure.

If there's still no movement after your first call, follow up again—firm, grounded, and clear.

Script: Holding the Boundary

> "Hi [Client Name], I noticed the invoice we discussed has still not been settled and wanted to check in again and make sure we can keep things moving without disruption."

WHY THIS WORKS

Anchors accountability and keeps the door open. It says: I see this. I'm not flinching. Let's resolve it so our working stays intact.

Let's move onto the how to handle when a client refuses to pay.

When a Client Refuses to Pay

Sometimes you'll do everything right and still end up chasing money.

When that happens, your body might brace. Your field might tighten. This is the moment to hold your structure—not collapse it. This is where you hold your structure—*no matter how messy the dynamic gets.*

Let me show you what this looked like in real life. We were handling bookkeeping for a marketing agency when they restructured their operations—requiring a brand-new accounting file.

We built it.

Even though it technically replaced the original file, we ended up maintaining both for nearly six months. Same transaction volume, double the work.

we didn't bill for the extra setup or volume—telling ourselves it was part of the transition

Meanwhile, they brought in an outsourced fractional controller.

They never engaged us directly, but we felt the undercurrent. Tension. Undermining. Passive resistance that started to wear on the relationship.

Eventually, it became clear: This wasn't going to work. We initiated off-boarding.

Then I sent the final invoice—for the new file and the transition work that had never been accounted for.

They refused to pay it.

I told them calmly and directly, that I couldn't release the new file until the outstanding balance was resolved.

They pushed back. I didn't flinch.

This wasn't about being difficult. It was about anchoring the integrity of the work—and protecting the value of our services.

They never paid. We kept the file.

Consistency Is Your Liberation

The real power in payment systems isn't protection—it's *liberation*. When your structure is clear, consistent, and upheld without apology, you stop spending valuable energy second-guessing, chasing, or over-explaining.

You don't have to hope someone pays you.

Your structure is your signal. Visibility is what makes it land. This consistency builds trust—with clients and also yourself.

Set it once. Say it clearly. Then let it live.

That's how you build a business rooted in respect—for your time, your energy, and your agreements. That's how you stop carrying the emotional weight of what you were never meant to chase. That's how you become the kind of business owner whose boundaries are never in question.

Reframing: Shifting Your Perspective on Getting Paid on Time Without Awkwardness

You've built the structure. You've clarified the expectations.

Now it's time to clean up any lingering beliefs that pull you out of clarity.

If you still feel resistance around follow-up or enforcement, it's not a strategy problem—it's a story problem. Rewrite the story.

Underlying Belief

If I follow up on an outstanding payment, the client will think I'm a nag.

New Perspective

Clients who value my work will respect my policies.

Having inconsistent rules doesn't attract the aligned clients, it attracts those who test boundaries.

Mindset Shift

Standing firm in my payment policy helps me build a business that is sustainable, profitable, and rooted in mutual respect.

Affirmation

I confidently communicate my payment terms and trust my clients to meet them.

KEY TAKEAWAYS

1. *Your payment process is a boundary.* It reflects how much you honor your energy, time, and value.
2. *Start with clarity.* Clearly state your payment terms in every agreement, invoice, and conversation.
3. *Never begin without the deposit.* Payment must be received before work begins to preserve the energetic exchange.
4. *Follow up without flinching.* Neutral, timely reminders show you lead with professionalism, not apology.
5. *Enforce with integrity.* If payment is missed, pause work and communicate next steps with certainty.

CHAPTER 6

Boundaries Are a Business Practice

You've got to love cell phones—they do so much for us. At the same time, they infringe on your boundaries if you let them.

We started working with a client who was, let's say . . . high touch.

Everything was an escalation. Every email, every text, was sent with some version of: "This is urgent." Except it wasn't.

It was always urgent to *her*—never critical to the *work*.

She'd message me at all hours. Weekends. Days off. No regard for time zones, bandwidth, or boundaries. Her energy? You work for me. Figure it out.

For a while, I tolerated it. I tried to be accommodating. I rationalized her behavior as part of the transition from having this role in house to being outsourced.

Until I realized I wasn't running my business, I was reacting to someone else's chaos.

Eventually I'd had enough. After another round of demanding emails and late-night texts, I responded—firmly but professionally. I told her, clearly and directly that her behavior was unacceptable. We loved working with the rest of her team but if she continued treating us this way, we could no longer support her account.

She called me.

We spoke. She's been in line ever since. That moment taught me something I'll never forget:

Boundaries don't have to be harsh to be firm.

They don't need drama or defense. They need to be clear, consistent, and enforced.

> **If you don't define the parameters, you'll get dragged into someone else's.**

Before we map the structure of sustainable boundaries, let's name the field this chapter clears.

Energetic Block This Chapter Clears
- I don't want to come off as difficult.
- I want to be seen as helpful—even if it costs me.

- If I set strict boundaries, I'll lose clients.

This chapter debunks that being accessible equals being valuable. And it interrupts the pattern of emotional over-extension that slowly erodes your time, energy, and leadership.

Boundaries aren't just policies, they're frequency protectors.

They don't push people away—they invite the right people to respect you more deeply.

What You're Repatterning

You're no longer leaving your availability—and your energy—up to chance.

This chapter repatterns your relationship with boundaries, not as barriers, but as invitations. Invitations to clarity. To sustainability. To self-respect.

You're not shrinking your accessibility, you're elevating your professionalism.

Because when your boundaries are clear, your value deepens not just in the work you do, but in the way you're received. This is where your "yes" starts to mean something again.

Field Calibration Before You Begin

Pause.

Breathe.

Close your eyes.

Recall the last time a client crossed a line—called after hours, ignored your process, or sent you spiraling with a passive-aggressive message.

Feel how your body responded. Notice what your body *wanted* to say but didn't.

This chapter puts that truth into structure.

You're not here to react, you're here to lead. Leadership begins with clear terms, clean agreements, and the willingness to be unavailable when necessary.

> **Your peace is part of your profit.**

You don't wait for alignment—you develop it from the first interaction.

Why Setting Boundaries Makes You a Better Service Provider

The strongest relationships in business are built on clarity, not confusion.

Every time you waffle on your availability, bend your process to be flexible, or say yes when your body is saying no, you dilute your power and confuse the client.

Clients thrive when they know the rules of engagement.

When you set clean boundaries, you:

- Create predictable, safe parameters.
- Set the tone for mutual respect.

- Protect your energy so your actual work can shine.

Boundaries don't make you rigid, they make you reliable.

They let the best version of you do the job you were hired to do—without resentment, depletion, or blurred lines.

One of my favorite quotes is from singer and actress Julie Andrews:

"Discipline gives me the freedom to fly."

That's exactly what boundaries do—they create a clear runway for everyone involved to move with ease and confidence. Most people like to know what's coming. Who doesn't love a good movie trailer?

Think of boundaries as your preview. They don't spoil the story, they make it easier for everyone to say yes to what's ahead.

What Not to Do
- *Don't say "I'm always available" unless you want to be.*
- *Don't reply to client messages at all hours unless you're being paid for 24/7 access.*
- *Don't let guilt write your response. Boundaries built from guilt collapse under pressure. The ones built from clarity? They hold.*
- *Don't assume clients know your availability unless you've explicitly stated it.*

- *Don't bend your policies to prove you're helpful.* Clarity is more valuable than over-functioning.

Set the Rules of Engagement Early

You teach your clients how to work with you from the first interaction.

If you respond to emails at all hours, always say yes to urgent requests, or let them skip steps in your process, you're silently erasing your boundaries while being helpful.

The fix? Set your operating rhythms *before* the work begins.

Think of this as your Client Operating Manual—a clear, calm set of expectations that allows your client to relax because they know exactly how and when you'll show up for them.

This includes:

- Your working hours
- Your average response time for emails or messages
- The holidays you take off (every year, no negotiation)
- Whether or not you check messages after hours or on weekends
- What to do if something's genuinely urgent (and how to define that)

You're not a 24/7 hotline. You're a business with a sacred rhythm.

Setting these boundaries upfront doesn't make you cold, it makes you clear.

> **Clients respect clarity more than constant availability.**

Once you've outlined your rhythms and expectations, it's time to communicate them—early, clearly, and with confidence. That way, there's no confusion down the line, and everyone knows exactly how the relationship will function.

Here's how I share with clients.

Script: "Here's How I Work"

"I'm available during [your working hours] and I typically respond to emails within [your standard timeframe]. I take off [your nonnegotiable holidays or days], and I don't monitor messages outside of working hours so I can be fully present when we are working together.

"If anything genuinely urgent comes up, here's how to flag it: [insert your escalation process, if any]."

WHY THIS WORKS

This structure helps me support clients with clarity, presence, and consistency. Most clients find it creates a smoother, more focused working relationship.

You've set the rhythm. You've communicated the rules.

Now comes the part most service providers struggle with: holding those boundaries without guilt.

How to Protect Your Energy Without Feeling Guilty

Most service providers know they *need* boundaries, but they struggle to hold them without guilt. That's because somewhere along the way, you learned to equate your value with your availability.

That being responsive = being reliable. That accommodating = being kind. That saying yes = being professional.

Let's untangle that now.

You don't protect your energy to be selfish. You protect your energy so you can do your best work. So you can show up clean, clear, and consistent. So you can stay in the game for the long haul—without burning out, over-giving, or silently resenting your clients.

Protecting your energy starts with:

- Being honest about your capacity.
- Saying no when it's not a full yes.
- Letting people down without letting yourself down.

And here's the magic: You can do all of that without apology.

Here's how.

Script: I'm at Capacity

> "I'd love to help, but I'm at capacity right now.
> If that changes, I'll be sure to let you know."

WHY THIS WORKS

This works because it's simple, kind, and clear. No over-explaining. No emotional labor. No guilt sandwich. Your job is to guard your time like you guard your energy—because they're one and the same.

Let me show you what it looks like when a yes costs more than a check ever could.

I was working with a small magazine that was struggling. I liked the young man—smart, well-funded—who was running it but the business model was never going to work.

When it became clear they'd have to shut down, he asked me to help with the wind-down. He promised I'd be paid before they closed. My schedule was already at capacity and this would take me over the edge of that.

My gut said no. I said yes anyway. I prioritized their needs. I turned work around quickly. Then—silence. The phone was disconnected. I got a generic letter saying there was no money to pay me. He walked away with $20,000.

I got nothing. That moment recalibrated me. Saying yes when your body says no isn't kindness. It's self-betrayal. And it's expensive.

Saying No to Free Work or Favors

Once you've clarified your capacity, the next step is protecting the scope. Because over-giving doesn't show up in your calendar—it shows up in the quick favors and one-more-thing asks that quietly stretch your container beyond what was agreed.

You're not a vending machine. You're not on call. Your value isn't measured by how much unpaid labor you give away.

Whether it's "Can you just take a quick look at this?" or "Can you squeeze in one more thing?" Every unspoken yes chips away at your clarity, your time, and your self-respect.

To be clear—we're not talking about resending a file or answering a simple yes/no questions. This isn't about being rigid. This is about honoring your scope.

Like when a client buys a headshot package and then asks for a custom social media banner. That's not part of the deal. That's a new ask—a new ask deserves new proposal, contract, or negotiation.

Here's the truth:

Every time you say yes to free work, you train your client to bypass your boundaries. You devalue your own expertise. You teach them that access is free— and that expectation grows quietly but quickly.

> **Saying no doesn't mean you're unhelpful.**
> **It means you're professional.**

It means you offer clear pathways for support—within the parameters of the relationship, not outside it.

Script: That's Not Something I Offer

> "That's not something I offer,
> but here's how I can help..."

WHY THIS WORKS
You redirect without guilt. You preserve the relationship *and* your integrity. You stop resentment before it starts.

Reframing: Shifting Your Perspective on Boundaries Without Guilt
Now that boundaries are defined and your scope protected, let's clear the emotional residue that can still linger. If guilt is running the show, even the best boundaries won't hold.

Underlying Belief
If I say no, I'll disappoint the client or lose the relationship.

New Perspective
Aligned clients aren't turned off by boundaries, they're drawn in by them. Clarity isn't rejection. It's leadership.

Mindset Shift

My boundaries build trust, not block connection. They create the spaciousness I need to do my best work, without depletion or resentment.

Affirmation

I honor my time, energy, and capacity with clear, grounded, unapologetic communication. The right people meet me there.

KEY TAKEAWAYS

1. *Boundaries are a service, not a shield.* They support the quality of your work and the sustainability of your energy.
2. *Clarity creates safety.* Clients relax and respect you more when they know what to expect.
3. *Define your availability.* Set and share your communication windows, response times, and escalation protocols clearly.
4. *Just because you're reachable doesn't mean you're available.* Protect your off-hours with the same intention you give your working time.
5. *No is not a rejection, it's refinement.* It redirects the energy back into aligned service and honors the parameters you've set.

CHAPTER 7

It's Okay to Renegotiate

At some point in your client relationships, something will shift. Maybe the work deepens. Maybe the scope stretches. Maybe the original rate no longer reflects the time, energy, or value you're bringing to the table.

Yet instead of initiating a new conversation, you hesitate. You keep over-delivering. You tell yourself, "It's just easier to leave it as is." You feel the tension—but don't want to rock the boat. Because the voice in your head says:

- "I don't want to bring up money again."
- "They've been with me so long. I feel bad changing the terms."
- "I already said yes, even though the work is no longer aligned."
- If I raise my rates or reset the scope, they'll leave."

These are echoes of an old pattern: keep the peace—even if it costs you. But peace built on suppression isn't peace—it's self-abandonment.

Here's the truth: Clarity is never the problem. Misalignment is.

Let's clear the energetic block that keeps you trapped in outdated agreements.

Energetic Block This Chapter Clears

You're not wrong for wanting more. You're not greedy, ungrateful, or demanding. You're evolving—and your agreements need to evolve with you.

This chapter clears the fear of rejection, scarcity-fueled loyalty, and the discomfort that comes with renegotiating money mid-relationship. It interrupts the pattern of over-delivery out of obligation, and restores your authority to lead the relationship as it grows.

What You're Repatterning

You are not here to shrink around your client's expectations. You are here to honor the *current truth* of the exchange.

This chapter repatterns the idea that agreements are fixed. They're not. They're living relationships. And as the energy shifts, so must the boundaries and investment.

You are allowed to grow. You are allowed to charge more when the work deepens.

You are allowed to say: "This is no longer sustainable and here's what needs to change."

When you trust your value, you stop conflating your prices with your identity. You stop fearing money conversations.

You stop tolerating agreements that no longer reflect the true scope or impact of your work.

This is where you shift from being accommodating to being a leader.

Field Calibration Before You Begin
Inhale.

Exhale.

Land in your body.

Let this knowing anchor you: You are not asking for permission to evolve. You are claiming the right to align your work, your value, and your agreements with the truth of who you are now.

You are not hard to please. You are no longer available for under-compensation. You are no longer shape-shifting to be easy to work with.

The more honestly you name what's true, the more powerfully the right people will meet you there.

How to Know When It's Time to Renegotiate
You don't need a crisis to justify change. You need clarity. Renegotiation isn't a reaction. It's a recalibration.

If something feels off in the exchange—if you're doing more than agreed, if the energy feels heavier, if your gut tightens before each call—it's time to check the field. Your discomfort is a signal of misalignment, not failure.

Here's what that can look like:

- The scope has crept. You agreed to X, but now you're also doing Y and Z—for the same rate.
- The hours have stretched. Calls run long. Slack is constant. You're mentally clocked in 24/7.
- The work has evolved. You're offering deeper strategy, emotional labor, or leadership—while still being paid for the starter version.
- The price no longer reflects your value. You've grown. Your expertise has sharpened. Your rates deserve to reflect that.
- The relationship is unbalanced. You're over-giving. They're under-acknowledging. You feel more like support staff than a strategic partner.

Any one of these is enough. You don't need all five. You don't need proof.

You don't need a script in hand before you're allowed to change course. You need to trust that your noticing is enough. Because it is. You're allowed to initiate the shift.

What Not to Do

- *Don't keep over-delivering and hope they'll just notice and offer to pay more.* Energetic martyrdom leads to resentment, not upgrades.
- *Don't let fear of rejection keep you in a misaligned agreement.* If it's draining you, it's already too expensive.
- *Don't tell yourself "it's not that bad" when your body knows it is.* Minimizing misalignment doesn't make it go away. It amplifies it.
- *Don't drop hints instead of having a direct conversation.* Clarity is kinder than ambiguity. Say what you mean. Name it.
- *Don't assume renegotiating will damage the relationship.* The right relationships adapt. The wrong ones reveal themselves.
- *Don't avoid the conversation because you don't have a perfect script.* You don't need perfect language—you need honest straightforward conversation.
- *Don't let scarcity convince you that this is the best you'll get.* That's not strategy. That's survival mode wearing a blazer. You're allowed to want more.

Renegotiation Begins With Honesty, Not Apology

> The renegotiation conversation isn't a confrontation. It's a recalibration.

It's not asking for more. It's naming what's true now. It's aligning the agreement with the actual energy, value, and deliverables you're bringing to the table—not the legacy version you outgrew six months ago.

Before you bring it to the client—bring it to yourself. Ask:

- Has the scope of work changed?
- Am I consistently over-delivering beyond the original agreement?
- Has the value I'm providing increased?
- Have my rates shifted since this client signed on?

Get honest, not defensive. Not over-explaining. Not waiting for perfect timing or permission.

This is not about their affordability. It's about your alignment. It's about whether the engagement still holds the truth of your current value. Because when it doesn't, you're the one suffering and that's not sustainable.

Once you're clear that something needs to shift, lead the conversation with calm authority. Make it a conversation, not just an email. These moments require presence. They deserve your voice, your energy, and your grounded leadership.

Script: Renegotiating With a Longtime Client

"I've taken some time to review our work together, and it's clear the scope has evolved beyond our original agreement. To ensure the relationship stays clear and sustainable, I'd like to update the way we're working together.

"Here are two paths forward:

[Option 1: The new offer/scope/rate that reflects the current scope of the work being performed.]

[Option 2: What stays the same—and what's removed to align with the original agreement.]

"Let me know which direction works for you. Either way, I'm committed to clarity, integrity, and a working relationship that works for both of us."

WHY THIS WORKS

It respects you, the client, and the relationship. You're not begging. You're not defending.

You're naming what's true, offering clear options, and honoring your growth without making the client wrong. It protects the relationship *and* your energy—by making sure both parties understand what's required to continue in alignment.

You're not saying *take it* or *leave it*. You're saying: Here's *what works now. Let's decide together what's next.*

When They Say No (or Flinch or Ghost)

Not everyone will meet you in your clarity and that's okay. That's the point.

Initiating a renegotiation gives the relationship a chance to evolve—or dissolve with integrity. If it can't? That's sacred information.

Some clients will push back. Some will quiet. Some will say, "I can't afford that."

Here's what you need to remember: Their response is never a verdict on your value. It's simply data about alignment.

When you're clear on what's aligned, you don't collapse to keep the peace. You hold the line with grace—because your leadership isn't up for negotiation.

You don't rush in with discounts. You don't backpedal to make it work. You hold the frame with calm leadership. You let them opt out, if they need to. And you trust that any space created will be filled with something better.

> **You are not for everyone.**

You are for the ones who respect the value you deliver. And if they push back? You don't need to prove, persuade, or defend. You hold the line with grace and decisiveness.

Script: Holding Firm After Pushback

> "I completely understand if this shift no longer fits your needs or budget. I care deeply about the integrity of the work, and I want to make sure we're both feeling aligned. If now's not the right time, that's OK. I'm still rooting for you."

WHY THIS WORKS

It protects the relationship without compromising your standards. It signals respect without self-abandonment. It lets the client exit with dignity—while you exit with your boundaries intact.

Reframing: Shifting Your Perspective on Rejection, Money, and Your Value

Let's pause and clear what might still be lingering beneath the surface. Even when you know you've renegotiated in clarity, even when the conversation has gone well—guilt can still echo. That's why boundary work isn't just external. It's internal repatterning too.

Underlying Belief

If a client says no, it means I asked for too much.

New Perspective

If a client says no, it simply means they weren't the match for the version of me I've become. Not every no is a loss—sometimes it's alignment doing its job.

Mindset Shift

Money discomfort usually isn't about the number. It's your inner protector bracing for rejection, judgment, or abandonment.

But you're not in danger. You're in expansion.

Affirmation

I trust that my value isn't determined by external validation. I am safe to grow, safe to charge, and safe to honor the evolution of my work.

KEY TAKEAWAYS

1. *Renegotiation isn't rebellion—it's refinement.* Agreements are living relationships, and as the energy shifts, so must the terms.
2. *Your noticing is enough.* You don't need proof to initiate a change. If something feels off, you're allowed to realign.
3. *Clarity is kinder than avoidance.* Naming the truth of your capacity creates trust, even if the outcome is a no.
4. *Your value doesn't hinge on who stays.* When you lead with integrity, the right clients rise to meet you and the misaligned quietly step back.
5. *Money conversations aren't dangerous.* They're invitations to honor your evolution, your energy, and the work as it lives now.

CHAPTER 8

Off-Boarding is Leadership

At some point, every client relationship reaches an end. The project wraps. The scope of work completes. Or you outgrow the dynamic.

Too many service providers ghost, shrink, or slip out quietly to avoid discomfort. But here's the truth: Endings are just as sacred as beginnings.

This chapter is your invitation to lead the full arch of the relationship—not just the exciting kickoff, but the quiet, necessary closure.

Whether it's a completion, a boundary, or a conscious uncoupling, it's time to normalize goodbyes that feel just as aligned as your hell yes, let's work together.

Energetic Block This Chapter Clears
- "I don't want to make it awkward."
- "If I say something, they'll think I'm ungrateful."
- "It's easier to just disappear or let it fade out."

This chapter clears the avoidance patterns that tend to surface at the end of a client relationship. It rewires the instinct to shrink, soften, or ghost. Instead, it restores your energetic posture to one of clarity and sovereignty.

What You're Repatterning
You're shifting from quiet exits to conscious completions. From loose ends to clean lines. From "I hope they don't notice" to "I honor this closure."

Off-boarding isn't just a formality. It's frequency work. It tells the Universe:
- I finish what I start.
- I close the loop.
- I integrate the energy.

This is professionalism that transcends transaction. This is maturity in motion.

Field Calibration Before You Begin
Breathe into your spine. Feel the weight of your integrity. You are not walking away. You are closing the circle.

Let your system ground into this truth:
- Clean endings are sacred.

- Clear communication is kind.
- Completion is magnetic.

Why Off-boarding Matters (Even If You Think It Doesn't)

Most service providers invest everything into onboarding. The welcome emails. The kickoff call. The burst of momentum.

But the end? Crickets. Silence. Or worse—avoidance.

Here's the truth: How you end a client relationship is just as important as how you begin one.

Your off-boarding process communicates:

- That you hold leadership through the full life cycle, not just when money is in motion
- That you honor the working relationship until the very last moment.
- That you clear the field before moving on.

A clean off-boarding says: This mattered. This was complete. My business has structure—and soul.

What Not To Do

- *Don't let the relationship fade out with no closure.*
- *Don't assume they know it's the last deliverable or session.*
- *Don't avoid sending the final invoice because "it's almost done anyway."*

- *Don't ghost instead of offering a handoff or referral.*
- *Don't over-apologize for boundaries or lack of future availability.*

Design Your Off-boarding Ritual

Off-boarding isn't admin, it's alchemy. It's a ritual. It's the intentional closure. It's a clearing of energy. It's a quiet exhale that makes space for your next expansion.

> Just like onboarding, off-boarding deserves structure, soul, and sovereignty.

Here's what a potent off-boarding ritual can include:

- Final deliverable recap: A clear list of what's been completed or handed off.
- Next steps or handoff instructions: Help them transition gracefully.
- Gratitude with boundaries: Thank them genuinely—without leaving the door wide open.
- Feedback invitation: A simple prompt while the experience is still fresh.
- Future pathways: If applicable, mention future offers or waitlists—no pitch, just possibility.

This isn't about clinging. It's about completing—with leadership.

Now that you've structured your closure, here's what it can sound like when communicated with clarity, gratitude, and grounded leadership.

Script: Off-boarding Email or Message

"Hi [Client Name],

"As we wrap up our work together, I wanted to take the time thank you. It's been a pleasure to support you through [brief mention of service or project].

"Here's a quick recap of everything we've completed:

- [Deliverable 1]
- [Deliverable 2]
- [Link to shared folders/resources]

"If any questions come up as you implement or transition, I'm available until [final availability date].

"I'm booked through [month], but I'll let you know if availability opens up in the future.

"If you'd like to share a testimonial, here's a simple form: [link]

"Thank you again for your trust—it means everything."

Why This Works:

It ends the relationship with warmth, clarity, and sovereignty—without lingering expectations or over-access. You're not over-functioning. You're closing the loop in a way that leaves both parties seen, respected, and free to move forward. Clean exits create space for aligned returns.

When you lead even your goodbyes with intention, you show the world you're here to start powerfully—and you're here to finish with grace.

Reframing: Completion Is Not Abandonment

Let's clear the internal static that can rise after a goodbye—even when the off-boarding is clean. Closure on paper doesn't always mean closure in the body.

Underlying Belief

If I don't stay accessible, they'll feel abandoned or they won't return.

New Perspective

Clients return when the experience is complete, not when access is indefinite.

Mindset Shift

Clean endings create space for new, aligned beginnings.

Affirmation

I close client engagements with clarity and grace, making room for what's next.

KEY TAKEAWAYS

1. *Off-boarding is energetic hygiene.* It clears the field and honors the full arc of the relationship.
2. *Closure is a part of the professional way you lead your business.* End with the same intention and integrity you began with.
3. *A clear process prevents confusion.* No assumptions. No open loops. No lingering questions.

4. *Goodbyes can build trust.* Clients remember how you made them feel—even at the end.
5. *You're not closing the door—you're sealing the chapter.* Completion isn't an ending. It's a beginning in disguise.

CHAPTER 9

This is the Beginning

You've walked through the frequency of clean money, clear communication, and sacred structure.

You've anchored a new standard—one where boundaries protect your brilliance, payments reflect your power, and process becomes the doorway to ease.

You now know:

- Boundaries aren't barriers, they're bridges.
- Payment isn't a transaction, it's an energetic exchange.
- Your process isn't admin, it's your authority in action.

Here's what you've embodied:

- You have a system for getting paid—clearly, consistently, and without apology.

- You know how to name your boundaries and hold them with love, not guilt.
- You lead money conversations with clarity, not contraction.
- You've swapped avoidance with alignment. Confusion with confidence.
- You've started speaking the language of money with sovereignty.

But this isn't the end. This is activation.

Now it's your turn to practice. Take the scripts. Make them your own.

Speak them out loud in front of a mirror. Try them in an email. In a voice note. On your next client call.

Feel what shifts in your nervous system when your words come from truth—not people-pleasing.

This work doesn't require perfection. It requires presence. And presence deepens through repetition.

The more you use these tools, the more embodied they become—and the more aligned your client relationships (and revenue) will feel.

You don't have to do this alone.

By reading this book, you've already stepped into a new paradigm—one where you speak up, get paid, and set the tone. Where clarity is the norm. Where energetic integrity leads.

This isn't a one-time recalibration. It's a lifelong practice.

Keep speaking.

Keep refining.

Keep leading.

Say the thing.

Set the boundary.

Raise the rate.

Close the loop.

Open the next chapter.

Money loves clarity.

And you, my friend, are now magnetic.

FINAL FREQUENCY LOCK

This wasn't a book, but a frequency shift.

You are no longer shrink around money. You move as its match. You are the sacred standard. Every boundary you set is a signal.

Every payment received is a reclamation. Every clear conversation is a line in the field.

I am no longer available for anything less than clean, true, sovereign exchange.

You did more than learn new language, you became a new frequency.

Remember:

- When you speak from power, your clients rise to meet you.
- When you name the truth, the right people lean in.
- And when you stay clean, the Universe pays in full.

Now go speak.

The world is listening.

Bonus Scripts for Sticky Situations

Clarity isn't always easy—but it's always powerful.

When fear, guilt, or awkwardness rise, don't freeze—speak.

Use these scripts as anchors—not to copy, but to calibrate. Let them remind your nervous system what truth sounds like in action.

When you don't know what to say, say:

Asking for the Deposit (Again)

> "Just a reminder that I'll need the deposit before we begin. Once that's received, I'll confirm your start date and lock in the timeline."

Following Up on Late Payment

> "Hi [Name], just circling back—looks like this invoice is still outstanding. Would you mind confirming the status on your end?"

Holding the Boundary When a Client Pushes It

> "Thanks for checking in! I'd love to help, but this falls outside the scope of our current work. Let me know if you'd like to expand the agreement or book a separate session."

Saying No to Free Work

> "That's not something I include in my current packages, but I'd be happy to share how we could add it if you're interested."

Protecting Your Time

> "I'm at capacity, so I'm unable to take anything else on right now. If that changes, I'll reach out."

Reinforcing Availability Hours

> "I'm available Monday through Thursday, 10 a.m.–4 p.m. I don't monitor messages outside those hours so I can be fully present when I'm working. I appreciate your understanding!"

Off-boarding With Elegance

"As our work together comes to a close,
I'll send over final notes and next steps. It's been
an honor supporting you—and if you need anything
in the future, here's how to stay in touch."

Redirecting a Scope Creep Request

"Thanks for your message. That sounds
like a great idea—it's not part of our current
agreement, but I'm open to expanding the scope.
Want me to send over an updated quote?"

The Money Conversation Seal

You made it to the end, but the
conversation is just beginning.

You've remembered truths that cannot be unseen.
You've touched codes that won't let you go
back. You've sat in sacred space with money
and maybe for the first time, *you stayed.*

Let this not be a finish line. Let
this be a frequency line.

Walk with what you now carry. Speak
from the clarity that met you here. Choose
from the power that rose in you.

You are no longer waiting for abundance.
You are co-creating with it.

The scroll is sealed.

The field is yours.

The conversation continues—every
time you choose to live it.

Want more support with pricing that actually holds?

From misaligned clients to wobbly numbers, the moments that shake your pricing are rarely about money alone. They're about boundaries, clarity, and the energy behind the conversation.

If you found *The Money Conversation* helpful, you'll love what's next.

Explore the Pricing Essentials Series — six short, practical workshops that help you align your pricing with your capacity, your energy, and the way you actually want to work.

You'll also find free trainings, real-world scripts, and other tools designed to make pricing feel less emotional — and more clear, calm, and sustainable.

Browse the workshops + resources here:

www.sumsolutions.com

About the Author

LINDA HUNT is the founder of SumSolutions and the author of *The Money Conversation: Speak the Truth. Set the Standard. Get Paid Without Apology.* She helps service-based entrepreneurs build wealth through structure, clarity, and intention—so their businesses support the results they deliver, without draining their energy.

With a background in corporate leadership and as one of the earliest pioneers in remote accounting services, Linda brings over two decades of experience at the intersection of numbers and nervous systems. Her work integrates financial clarity, operational integrity, and energetic alignment to help founders stabilize their systems, communicate with confidence, and build businesses they can actually hold.

At SumSolutions, Linda and her team deliver both done-with-you consulting and done-for-you accounting, supporting entrepreneurs with the structure required to scale sustainably—without self-abandonment, hustle, or burnout.

Her approach is rooted in the belief that calm, clear money conversations don't come from memorized scripts—they come from a business built in alignment with what it's here to do. When structure holds your standards, you don't have to prove your worth. You just show up in truth—and get paid accordingly.